Under the Equator

AUSTRALIAN STORIES THAT NEED TO SURFACE

JOHN JAMES

Ark House Press
arkhousepress.com

Some names and identifying details have been changed to protect the privacy of individuals.

Cataloguing in Publication Data:
Title: Under the Equator
ISBN: 978-1-7642813-0-0 (pbk)
Subjects: REL012170 RELIGION / Christian Living / Personal Memoirs

Cover image courtesy of Elliot Gray

Design by initiateagency.com

PREFACE

Under the Equator is a biographical journey focused on four couples across four eras (1850s – 1870s, 1920s – 1930s, 1950s -1960s and 1960s – recent). Their lives incorporate first generation experiences, Victoria's last frontier: The Mallee, changing ethos's, our drift to a coastal life and God in the midst of it all.

These generational stories are part of the landscape and deserve to be heard in that space which is; 'living an Australian life'.

I selected people whose lives I could give some credibility to and the details of which I could authenticate. Surnames have been omitted as these are stories for everyone and are not to be constricted to a family genealogy.

Their lives in some small way speak to the inter-connectedness of the Australian community. As such they deserve the respect of forebears who in their own way contributed to the welfare of the people of this land.

The stories have been kept short so readers of varying abilities who enjoy hearing or watching true stories may also engage with the people in this book.

Under the Equator is for my people who are now at eight generations and your people for however many generations you can count back.

TABLE OF CONTENTS

CHAPTER ONE

Late Spring.

The Southern Ocean yaws with the surge and thud of deep throated waves on any descent surf beach along the West Coast of Victoria. Mist fills the air with the scent of brine, seaweed and the possibilities of the deep reaching up from Antarctica. There are journeys to be made. Southern Right and Humpback Whales, Bottlenose and Burrunan Dolphins, Great White and Bronze Whaler Sharks, Yellowtail Kingfish, Southern Bluefin and Big Eye Tuna are on the move with a thousand other species intent on shorter travels.

But it's the smell, the smell of the ocean that fills your lungs and your heart with an ethereal sensation. It can breathe wholeness into you if you let it.

With a surfboard under your feet, you know you can both tame and work with what each wave writes on the surface of the deep.

* * * * * * * * * * * *

A few steps back up the beach and it is April 26 1852.

My ancestors have scored a trail across the Southern Ocean's surface on a 968-ton ship called the Garland with the guidance of the ship's master, William Halcrow. They sailed from Liverpool after travelling overland from the region of Gretna, Dumfriesshire, Scotland.

The Garland had been converted to carry 364 government emigrants. Then as now the government was trying to fill holes in the workforce. Australia needed agricultural labourers for the many vacancies on properties, created in the previous 20 odd years.

The colony of Victoria, established July 1 1851, desperately needed agricultural labourers.

The initial policy had been to seek single men for the work because of the tyranny of distance and the travel required to get to some properties. Single men had no-one to draw them away from remote locations, or so the theory went.

It didn't work. Being single also meant the men were a more mobile workforce.

Then gold came into the equation. First discovered in Clunes, near Ballarat, in 1850, the lure of gold was pulling single men to the alluvial fields of Victoria. A change of policy was required.

Let's promote Australia as a family destination and hopefully that will bring some stability to aspects of the economy other than gold, said Melbourne's business and political leaders.

Hence my ancestors came as government emigrants having dutifully lied to the officials by stating they were agricultural labourers. They were masons and joiners who knew some basics of animal husbandry, as did anyone coming from rural Scotland.

The first Australians in my family to come out of the European mist of time arrived in Hobson's Bay, Victoria.

Venturing further back in that European mist there is mention of our family's surname in various parts of Scotland and Ireland. Some were tenant farmers in the Lockerbie area.

Thank God they didn't remain there or we might have had Pan Am flight 103 drop on our heads in 1988.

Others were involved in varying import/export businesses, banking, trades or were school masters. The usual mixed bag of most families.

Then, in the mix, there is mention of two brothers, James (my direct forbear) and Thomas, who were involved with the Covenanters in the 1680's. This was not a good time to be a Presbyterian living in Scotland.

1679 – 1688 was dubbed 'the killing time'.

Fundamentally there was an Act of Parliament, 'the drunk parliament', in 1661 titled the Rescissory Act. This act effectively sacked 400 ministers in Scotland and forced a hierarchical system of government on the church. The church of Scotland had to accept any candidate presented to it by the crown or a patron.

Possibilities for political and vested interest appointments are glaring.

It can be confidently said that a lot of Scottish people saw this as a wolves dressed in sheep's clothing scenario, something Jesus warned about. It's not exactly the way to find good shepherds for Christs' followers.

The appointed bishops held seats in the Scottish Parliament, which brought that body back more into line with the English monarchy. Presbyterians, who largely rankled at this politicisation of the church, found life harder and harder.

James (Captain Long Gun) is recorded as the leader of a band of covenanters who attacked royal troops in the Pass of Enterkin and rescued a group of covenanters including his brother Thomas. Covenanters had vowed to uphold Presbyterian faith free of English, or any political interference.

It's 1684 and the royal troops were headed for Edinburgh, where the covenanters would stand trial.

Thomas was subsequently caught a second time, tried and executed for his involvement in the fracas. He was hung in the Grassmarket in Edinburgh. James managed to escape and went into exile with his family in Ireland for twenty odd years only returning to Scotland to live out his last days. Hence this branch left some family behind who became Irish.

Dubbed 'the killing time', my forbear Thomas, was just one of an estimated 18,000 people executed in Edinburgh over roughly a decade long purging of anyone the English deemed trouble.

If we venture even further back in that European mist of time, we can fairly confidently say our surname, which is a reference to a location, is an Anglicised version of a place in Norway.

Did that mob come down through the Shetlands, the Orkneys and the West Hebrides into Scotland. This is speculative conjecture but we were never a clan in Scotland.

Another theory hypothesises they came as Normans via England into Scotland. An early (1273) recording of our family surname places 'de' before it. Also, an early version of the family coat-of-arms has three fleur-de-leis. Norwegian Vikings to Normandy, to Great Britain could have been their movement.

And what of the great before. The general movement of tribes along migratory routes westward across Europe from the Middle East.

It is interesting to ponder but we will stick to the known in this tale...

... my people's First Australians and ensuing generations who call Australia home.

They arrived April 26 1852. A family of eight, having all survived the journey, had left the Northern Hemisphere for good. There was John (42), Janet (44), James (20), William (18), Edward (15), and Jesse, John and Janet all under 10.

John (the father) and his twin, David, were the youngest of five sons and so the youngest of that line was the first here.

He was the second John to arrive on these shores. The first came in 1839. Earlier, branches of the family had left Scotland for Canada and the U.S.A.

Australia was crying out for agricultural workers. The fact the family was sought, because their labour was valued, and could come, was due also to another policy change. Up until 1851 you could not bring three children under 10 to the colonies.

That would have been too much of a distraction from work commitments.

The colonies of Australia wanted workers not extra mouths to feed.

Now the door is wide open.

In the Garland's logbook they are listed as Presbyterians who could read and write, a highly desirable skill at that time, and now, in new migrants. Their basic education came from parish schools in this era, something that did not happen in England, Ireland or Wales.

My people also came on their 'own account'. What better migrants could you hope for than people who pay their own way. No government assistance, no passage paid by a business looking to contract you for x amount of time, meant they were free to go where they wanted and fundamentally follow their vocations in the bustling surge of new migrants chasing Victoria's gold.

They just had to survive the voyage.

95 days after sailing out of Liverpool the Garland docked in Hobson's Bay, as the top of Port Phillip Bay was then known. The Argus, an early Victorian newspaper, reported their safe arrival on August 2 1852. They came the standard route around the Cape of Good Hope into the Roaring Forties to slingshot across the Indian and Southern Oceans. Then they navigated Bass Strait and the shipwreck coast of Western Victoria.

This stretch of the great deep blue has huge swells that can readily toss and drive a ship onto hazardous reefs and coastline. Many a hope and dream never reached fulfillment because of the treacherous waters.

An early Scottish bookplate of the family motto has a ship tossed by the oceans. It seems someone had a prophetic awareness of what would happen across the generations with the family.

Was the Southern Ocean kind to them in July 1852?

July, especially, on the shipwreck coast can be wild. Did they plane through winter's green seas and note the passing of what became Portland, Warrnambool, Port Campbell and the Twelve Apostles (there probably were twelve then), Apollo Bay and Barwon Heads?

The Roaring Forties were a well-known sea path in the early 1850s unlike some sections of our coast. Surveys of the Australian coast were still being conducted, especially in the north, through the Torres Strait and around Cape York. The world was opening to Europeans but much was unknown and perilous.

Over 600 vessels did not survive the Southern Ocean and Bass Strait. Melbourne remained a port too far for them.

The Argus said 364 people arrived "in excellent health and condition" on the Garland, a strong indication everything went well on this trip. Captain William Halcrow safely transported 133 married couples, 47 single women, 58 single men, 48 boys under 14, 62 girls under 14 and 15 infants.

But there is more to the story than a generalisation.

The reality of a 95-day successful voyage in those waters in 1852 was 16 infants died 'from natural diseases and attendant on children' and three adults 'from general debility'.

To our ear the phrasing is not just archaic but matter of fact. Life was more tenuous and death, especially in your first years, often held the upper hand. Death just happens and no medical diagnosis can challenge, explain or clarify reasons for its' toll.

You simply died of 'natural diseases' and 'general debility'.

Life delivers up natural ('attendant') health issues which snatch your final breath.

There were also four births on the trip which says a lot about the mothers who were simply getting on with life no matter the circumstances. They were Australia bound and would deal with what happened along the way.

The family arrived and settled in Connewarre a stones throw from Barwon Heads and Thirteenth Beach.

Along a three kilometre stretch of Thirteenth Beach six vessels sunk in Bass Strait's tumultuous seas. The Earl of Charlemont, from which the reef off Barwon Heads Bluff gets its name, went down in 1853. Lady Harvey sunk off Beacon, the best surf break on Thirteenth, in 1858. Ant, which carries the name of one of the most westerly surf breaks on Thirteenth, went down in 1866. The other vessels were Anne, South Milton and Sussex.

So, what motivates a middle-aged couple with six children to leave everything known, and whose cultural mores inhabit the pores of their skin, to venture into the largely unknown? They weren't just middle-age, they had hit the average life expectancy for their respective sexes.

Janet's family are a question mark. John's father, James, had died in 1831 but his mother, Isabella, was 75 when they sailed.

Other members of the family would have to look after his aging widowed mother. She lived to 93, an extraordinarily long life for the era, dying six years after her son John died on the other side of the world. It is quite likely she never knew anything of what happened to her family on these shores.

Literacy did not ensure communication with the other side of the world.

There is an interesting aside here as James and Isabella had our people's surname before they were married. Yep. It happened. Second cousins? The families lived within a small radius of a few fields in the Dumfriesshire and marriage within an extended family was not uncommon.

Another titbit regarding Isabella is she was baptised eight months after her parents married. I am sure you have already done the maths.

That might have created a bit of drama in the family and community, although it was far from being unique.

For John, Janet and children, Scotland did not hold out a future with any real hope for tradesmen.

Two converging vortexes were occurring.

The 'clearances' in Scotland in the 1840s and 1850s changed the face of the country. Tennant farmers were being evicted in large numbers. Those who could afford it were looking for larger swathes of land to make it more profitable to run sheep. This resulted in large numbers of dispossessed and instituted the steady breakdown of the clan system.

Alongside the social breakdown were potato famines. Blight had wreaked havoc with potato crops since 1846. The dangers of heavy dependence on a monoculture were laid bare. One glitch with a 'nasty' and famine looms large.

Potato famines were not confined to Ireland.

With destitution rife, Scotland, my forbears decided, had little to offer. Despite their age, 1852 was the right year for John and Janet to pack the little they had and go.

Adventure was not part of their suitcase of motives for striking out. They knew no-one here. It was a case of go with their Presbyterian hope and faith and see if life can't be better for all eight of them.

On arrival the family made its way from Melbourne to Geelong away from the flow of traffic heading to the goldfields.

The Garland, on returning to England, set sail again on December 28 1852. She sailed for Amoy in the Fukien province of China.

Perhaps Captain Halcrow saw a quicker profit to be made in bringing perspective Chinese gold miners to Victoria, before returning to Liverpool.

'China was the future', at least in the short term, for the Garland.

That sounds like a catch-phrase for Australian trade today, although we are currently looking for more diversification.

John, Janet and the six children settled in the Mt. Duneed region twelve kilometres south of Geelong where suburban sprawl has just about reached the graves of my first two ancestors in Australia. A mossy headstone still speaks their names in the Presbyterian section of Mt. Duneed cemetery.

With hindsight, it is amusing but sad to note each denomination had their own section in this and many cemeteries. I recall Jesus saying in my father's house there are many rooms and I go to prepare a place for you. There is definitely no place for segregation in that big household.

The family got to work doing what they knew, building. Family tradition has it they had a hand in the construction of certain bluestone bridges, houses and schools in the region.

The Geelong Advertiser records Edward, the third son, made improvements to the Newtown State School residence and added an extra classroom in the 1870s.

Beyond a few sketchy details their lives merged into the landscape. There was still no country called Australia when they died. They lived their later years in a colony.

John had a decade on this soil while Janet had three decades. They saw money flood into Victoria via the gold rush. The economy went from virtual insolvency to wealthy. Geelong benefitted from the gold of Ballarat, Bendigo and lesser regions.

Wealth created work for the family.

In their time fellow Scotsman James Harrison, founder of the Geelong Advertiser, invented refrigeration. The first country railway in Australia, between Melbourne and Geelong was opened in 1857 and five years later the Geelong – Ballarat line opened. Wool began to fill the wool stores being built in Geelong, for sales and shipping, largely to England. And gas came to Geelong in 1860.

These developments were part and parcel of their experience in a new world, a different world.

As first-generation migrants it is hard to say to what extent the land had worked its' way under their skin but there was no other life for them. Australia was home. Their children, especially the youngest three, largely knew nothing but this soil and the Southern Ocean.

When it came time to bury them in Wathaurong soil, we find their age on their headstones doesn't match the Garlands' records. Janet died August 30 1884 aged 78. John died 1864 aged 57.

Janet's headstone reads: 'Whose anxious prayer in life was; So, sitting at Thy feet would all His love outpour. And pray Thou wouldst teach me Lord to love Thee more and more.' Faith and love carried Janet through a turbulent life in a new world.

Some of that turbulence is spelt out in the nature of her husband's death. John's headstone only says he was a mason but the coroner's inquest into his death paints a little more of the direction his life took in the Victorian colony.

Firstly though, the headstone. Epitaphs from this time are interesting because they were often penned by those close to the deceased rather than being the deceased's words. All the family could say about John was what he did for a living. Nothing personal. Nothing complimentary. Nothing about how he lived life.

It would be foolish to pass judgement 160 years after the event but that one word is stark on his headstone.

So how did he die?

Why was a coroner's inquest warranted?

John may well hold the unenviable epitaph of being the first person to be killed in a drink driving accident on a Victorian road.

The inquest into his death presided over by Forster Shaw, as reported in the Geelong Advertiser, was held the afternoon of the accident at the Bay View Hotel in Germantown.

An inquest in a pub? Does that not sound a little bit so Australian.

Can you imagine the legal machine today getting witnesses and the coroner together with a decision made the day of an accident.

Oh, for a more streamlined legal system.

Germantown was settled by several German families, in 1849, who made some early attempts at viticulture in the region. It was renamed Grovedale (now a suburb of Geelong) in 1915 due to anti-German sentiment whipped up by WW1.

There were four people called to give testimony, at the Germantown pub. A neighbour, two publicans and a policeman.

The neighbour, John Smart, heard a spring cart pass his farm about 11 o'clock the previous night. When he went to fetch his horse at 4am, to go into Geelong, he noticed a chestnut horse by the road. On checking he found two men, one slightly on top of the other, lying on the road. One, with a whip in his hand, was dead. The other he 'shook' for some time before he could 'rouse' him.

He had lain unconscious on the road for hours.

The pair had been thrown some yards from the cart and lay where they fell. John had bled profusely from his mouth and nose.

The spring carts' shaft and bellyboard were broken when the cart hit a pile of stone on the roads' edge. Ironically, the 'metal' was dropped off for road maintenance with the view to making the road safer.

Their horse, characterised as 'restive' by neighbours, was clearly travelling with enough speed to launch John and Edward.

The last people to see them alive were publicans Albert Benari and Felix Mulholland.

John went into Albert's pub, hatless and intoxicated, looking for a drink the evening of the accident. Albert had known John for eight years. He refused to give him whiskey but gave him a pipe to smoke and then sent them on their way.

Edward, being in a worse state than his father, had stayed in the cart.

The second pub they went to in Germantown was Felix's. Felix had known John for about 12 years, basically since they had arrived in the colony, and claimed he often saw him much drunker than this night. This was probably true even though there was motivation to distance himself from the accident.

John and Edward had a 'little' gin in some peppermint and continued on from Felix's pub.

The family had been in Australia 12 years and it appears John arrived on these shores with an alcohol problem. Alcoholism begs the question how did the family manage financially over those 12 years. It also raises additional questions about motives for migrating.

In leaving Scotland were John and/or Janet looking to remove alcohol from John's life?

The constable who arrived at the scene at 5:30am was Michael O'Hare. He noted a rear wheel of the cart hit the stone ('metal') and the horse, having fallen, was on its feet again.

John was dead and Edward 'seemed stupid', said Constable O'Hare.

Quite the medical diagnosis.

Shock and concussion were still playing out when Edward was taken to hospital in Geelong.

Edward obviously came to his senses again as he was the one extending Newtown State School some seven to nine years after the accident.

A drink-driving death always has repercussions for a family.

John's fourth son, also John, became an elected trustee of the Rose of Australia Union Daughters of Temperence in 1871, a group who encouraged their men, in particular, to be non-drinkers. Other family members would also have stories to tell about their father's death if only they could.

Edward recovered from being 'seemingly stupid' and continued building in the Geelong region but having laid with his dead father that horrible night, his would be the most interesting story to hear.

John wasn't the only early family member to die on Victoria's roads. In 1929 Andrew died after being skittled in a hit and run in Melbourne.

How you manage a getaway after a car accident in 1929 fuels the imagination. Not to deny the horror of what took place, it is hard to shake images of the Keystone Cops, from the early days of the movie industry, buffooning their way through another misadventure.

John and Janet didn't have the best of starts to life in Australia but from Connewarre, where Janet resided on a small farm until her death, their descendants have spread out across Australia to the tune of eight generations.

CHAPTER TWO

With the movement of family, we now step forward to Robert Roy (Roy) and Ellen (Nell). Roy got the full moniker despite being fourth generation Australian.

How Scottish can you get!

At least it was a change from James or John. There have been a lot of Johns in the family. (Yes, there is humour in that line.)

Roy and Nell's working and personal lives are somewhat indicative of their generation.

Firstly, though, a brief tale of Nell's mob.

Nell's paternal grandparents were from England. He was a gunsmith who hawked his trade around the Victorian goldfields in the 1850s-1860s.

This was a time when you could make a viable living from 'gunsmithing'.

Victoria was a raw new colony and concerns around personal safety on the goldfields, where a lot of money was being made, did not involve total reliance on the constabulary.

From the goldfields he made the career move to farming at Kooreh, near St Arnaud, Victoria.

The oldest son, Nell's father's brother, was deaf and dumb, as defined then.

Trained as a tailor in Melbourne, he seldom, and reluctantly, took up needle and thread thereafter. He preferred to do the wheelwright work on the farm with some occasional piece work making flannel underclothes. Producing piece work clothing from home probably paid as poorly as it often does today.

This extended family, uncle and in-laws, were part of Nell's early childhood. They lived next door to them in a two-room mud brick house. Nell's home was grander being a four-room mud brick dwelling. For the early 1900s it was very rudimentary housing.

Nell's maternal grandparents came from Scotland. After sailing for three months, they docked in Adelaide. From there they journeyed overland by bullock wagon the 550 kilometres to St. Arnaud.

It is not clear why they stepped ashore in Adelaide only to head to Victoria. Perhaps there was a relative already in Adelaide.

They definitely weren't Chinese.

In the middle 1850s the Victorian government was concerned about conflict on the goldfields between Europeans and Chinese. Their political solution was to introduce measures to make it less profitable to bring Chinese to the colony with a tax imposed on each person and a limit on how many Chinese any ship could carry.

Ship owners dodged these measures by docking in Adelaide or Robe, South Australia. The Chinese then walked to Ballarat, Bendigo etc with the help of a paid guide.

Nell's grandparents would have required a guide also but the goldfields were not on their radar. They came to farm and they established themselves in the Wimmera.

Her parents met and married in Geelong. When Nell was six, they moved to Maryborough. Herbert (Bert), Nell's father established a furniture removalist business carting with horse and wagon the 550 km round trip between Melbourne and Maryborough. On average the journey would take him a week. Winter roads being far worse for horse and skinny wagon wheels, and for her father who would camp with his load, could take longer.

He was the equivalent of a long-haul trucker or removalists who do the Victoria to Queensland run only to return some house lots to Victoria sometime later.

Overall, work was too inconsistent though. At one point the grocer cut their credit as they owed 30 shillings ($280 today). The baker kept them going when finances were tight. Consequently, some meals they sat at the table and only had bread and suet for tea.

Great diet. Not.

Without a welfare system to support you when you hit financial trouble you would just muddle through as best as you could. Life bred independence in you. Besides you were not the only family in this situation.

When her father had work, he was gone for days so her mother became the one to exercise discipline in the family. Nell described her mother as a bit like her… 'a plump, dumpy little lady but very nice. She was down-to-earth and generous.'

Being down to earth seems to be a quality Australians have admired for generations.

'Generous' is quite an amazing choice of descriptors given the life they led. To be generous of spirit is an admirable trait and to maintain that spirit when poor is even more admirable.

Despite some erratic work patterns, for a few years, Nell said her father was … 'a hard worker and honest. He helped people who had 'troubles' and his word was law, although he was not bossy.

She also attested to that wonderful Australian understatement… 'he was an average man who drank an occasional glass of beer.'

The family moved on to Tempy, in the Victorian Mallee, to a farm with a two-room corrugated iron shack sitting on top of a sandhill. They carted water to pack and smooth down a mud floor. Cut hessian bags were laid across the compacted dried mud as a carpet of sorts.

The home was not Grand Designs Australia chic. Construction belonged to an earlier era than their 1910-1920 timeframe spent living in it. Housing in rural Victoria was well behind more established towns and cities.

Such were the times in the Mallee, the frontier Northwest corner of Victoria.

In 1915 there was a particularly bad mouse plague. Nell recalled babies in cradles being strung from the roof by wire to stop mice nibbling on them. This was part of the mix in a frontier life.

Saturday night dances and Sunday morning church was where troubles were dispensed and joy expressed. Bert continued to play the accordion at local dances.

Nell could dance before she was 12 years old.

The norm at the Tempy Saturday night dances was dancing on one side of the barn with horses feeding on the other side. At least the horses helped cover body odour, especially in the warmer months. Horse odour? That was another thing altogether.

Roy met Nell and Nell met Roy in Tempe. I like to think they were a Saturday night dance hookup which lasted for fifty years. In the days of chaperones, it would have been handy having Bert as the accordion player.

Roy was from a farming background although his father did work as a wood merchant in Melbourne for a while. He was working on extensions to the irrigation channels in the Mallee in the early 1920s.

Working with draught horses he fashioned and smoothed the new channels.

The government of the day was very keen to turn the Mallee scrubland into a food source for the state. Water needed to be pushed further out from river systems to see if this was viable land.

More country had to be opened up.

Mallee irrigation schemes were initiated back in the 1880s by Alfred Deacon, who was later to become our Prime Minister on three occasions.

By the 1920s people were a little more aware of salinity issues and the destructive habits of yabbies on the channels. Some improvements in construction were instituted.

Around this time the Soldier Settlement Scheme was under way. Returned servicemen, nurses, or widows, mothers or children of deceased WW1 soldiers were eligible for a land grant.

700 properties were offered in the Mallee through this scheme making it the largest single development of any Soldier Settlement Scheme in the country.

Many returned soldiers, and there were 78,000 in Victoria, were unemployed.

Land was a thank-you for your service and an opportunity for a livelihood.

W.W.1. veterans could not choose a land lot nor was there a house on any of the properties. Government help extended to offering establishment loans and advising on livestock purchases, farming equipment etc.

Unfortunately, many who took up land were not in a position financially, physically or mentally to cope with the harsh conditions of the Mallee. An unknown number shot themselves and by 1939 60% had walked off their land.

There were far too many personal tragedies unseen and quickly forgotten in the heat and sand.

The state, in the short term, took an economic hit also.

This was when Roy and Nell took up farming.

Roy and Nell did not acquire land through the Soldier Settlement Scheme. Both were born in 1900 and hence missed any involvement in WW1.

The government, very keen for Mallee land to be put to agricultural use, also provided another access point, the Closer Scheme. This second scheme was to ensure as much land as possible was being taken up.

Roys' experience in the Mallee, working on the new irrigation channels, paved the way for them to take on a freehold section of Mallee scrub. The details of this arrangement are lost but the upshot was they took possession of 500 acres of bush at Karween in 1927.

Karween, 200 kms northwest of Tempe, and a little north of the Sunset Country, was new territory for them. Whether they had any choice in selecting the land is doubtful. Like the returned soldiers you got what you got.

Nell, having lived in the Mallee for a dozen years, and Roy having worked in the region, were better prepared for what lay ahead of them than were the vast majority of ex-servicemen.

Just getting to Karween was quite the journey. Having married in 1923 and now with two young boys (which was to grow to six) in tow, Nell loaded their few essentials on a wagon, tied a gig behind and set off.

Roy was already on the property with his brother Andrew, having commenced the work of clearing Mallee scrub.

Nell could only manage 29kms a day because the road was sandy and in terrible condition. With two little boys to attend to it took a week to get there despite harnessing up the horses at dawn each day.

The Karween property had a bush shanty on it.

This leads me to speculate it might have been a Soldier Settlement block which someone had walked off. Maybe that is why some properties under the Closer Scheme were being offered to channel irrigation workers and others with experience in the Mallee.

The shack had hessian walls and a roof of four-gallon tins of honey and flour, cut and spread across the sapling rafters.

Nell and Roy added a second room to the hut and collected empty kerosine tins from the channel works to fashion a chimney and walls. A corrugated iron roof replaced the existing one. Bush beds, made from hessian sacks, were strung between poles. There was no fly wire.

This was to be home for 18 months. In summer it was so hot you did all of your cooking outside on an open fire. Water had to be carted from the government dam in Karween as there was none on the property when they took possession.

A bush block is a bush block.

Washing was boiled and beaten in a tub outside and strung up in the dusty air to dry.

None of this was a new experience for Nell. She was already battle hardened.

Karween was their opportunity to own and work something for themselves and they threw themselves into the task at hand with all the enthusiasm and optimism of the young at heart.

Initial tasks were to clear land and dig a dam. Carting water from the government's Karween dam was time consuming and limited. Most of the Mallee scrub was felled by axe and eventually 150 of the 500 acres was cleared for dry cropping wheat.

Their first crop was small and poor.

This was subsistence living.

A stable was built for the draught horses, an enclosure for pigs and a pole shed for two milking cows. The chickens, which usually numbered around 50, roosted in two peppercorn trees. That meant eggs could go undetected and become a great weapon for a growing number of boys. They had an incubator which hatched 20 chicks at a time.

There were no foxes killing off free ranging chickens or causing other problems.

The most problematic animal was their boar if it managed to bail you up. Mice plagues and rabbit plagues created their own set of headaches.

At the other end of the animal kingdom were their pets, blue-tongue lizards and hand reared magpies.

In 1928 they took possession of a small four room weatherboard house built for them by the Victorian government as part of the

Closer Scheme. The home would house eight people, nine on occasion when a single female teacher at the Karween Primary School boarded with them.

They were to become the first people in Karween to have a phone in the house.

Life was on the up for the region as more people were able to move from a humpy into housing.

But the Mallee has a way of keeping you stoic with your nose to the grindstone and in 1928 they faced their first serious dust storm. Nell said you could not see your hand even when you held it up in front of your face.

In more recent times, 1983, we had a literal taste of Mallee dust when soil was blown half way across Victoria to swallow Melbourne and Port Phillip Bay. Grit found its' way between your teeth and an eerie world ensued with dust in your eyes and every other orifice.

Even back in the 1920s there was erosion problems in the Mallee.

Mallee gum (the local indigenous word is mali) has a prodigious root network which holds together the friable sandy soils of the region.

The government required all Settlement properties to maintain native bush boundaries. This was not always adhered to so when you combine vegetation reduction with a dry season you get liftoff.

Sand dunes became mobile.

Their boys, attending the local primary school five kilometres away could find themselves walking home barefoot through a different landscape after a day at school. Fences clearly visible in the morning were no longer so. Tracks could change significantly. It was like a fog.

They sought out shelter behind trees, for a break from sand cutting their legs and their feet sinking into scalding sand. This also was part of life as they knew it.

Life wasn't all hardship though and a bush school can provide memorable days foreign to towns and cities.

On Melbourne Cup Day a teacher would take the kids across the railway yards to Pop's shop to listen to a radio and buy lollies. For Guy Fawkes night, November 5, everyone gathered at school for a large bonfire. On other occasions they made boats to float in the channels on the annual run and swam in dams when the teacher deemed it hot enough to take them.

On the flip side Grade 6 boys had the Friday afternoon task of burying 'Willie' (the outside dunny cans) in the schoolyard.

Their only drink at school was from a waterbag hanging in a gum tree with one mug attached to it, a far cry from students having water bottles sitting on their desks today.

A version of bush medicine remained the norm for the 13 years Nell and Roy spent in Karween. You sprinkled pepper on bleeding cuts, rinsed sore eyes with boracic acid, took eucalyptus with sugar or lemon juice, or honey and aspirin for coughs, and stomach complaints got a good dose of castor oil or Epsom salts.

Meanwhile Roy continued to pull stubborn stumps from the ground with his six draught horses and plant a further few acres of wheat. There were always Mallee stumps around the property as fencing for yarding and for fuel.

Neighbours depended on neighbours throughout these years. Without some sense of community people wouldn't have coped.

Isolation can be suffocating.

Five of the boys were born in Mildura and one in Renmark. Nell would head off two weeks before she was due and stay with a relative. Mildura was a 110km trip and Renmark was 70km from Karween.

Travel had its' challenges on rudimentary tracks over such distances.

Nell would return two weeks after each birth. This was her break away from the property and a well-earned one at that.

Saturday night, like many country regions, was dance night. Karween dances were a social life force for the community. When they could the family would jump in their Model-T Ford and hit the dance floor. The youngest boys were left in the car to sleep. It had no windows but the boys felt secure sleeping in it.

It all sounds suspiciously like leaving kids in a pub carpark while mum and dad play the pokies and/or drink. The difference is in Roy and Nells' era there was no implication or stain of negligence and there were no safety issues.

A new era was emerging. Horses no longer took up half of the dance hall.

Progress.

Semi regular contact on the farm also came in the form of a grocer who travelled the district.

Mildura was a world away and it was a metropolis in the boys' eyes.

On Sunday the school room was used for church and Sunday School, a spiritual and a social gathering.

In 1931 Roy and Nell had their first bumper wheat crop after struggling for four years. It proved to be just as frustrating as the poor harvests. The Great Depression was biting and wheat prices plummeted.

This story was retold a second time in the Depression. Then came the drought of 1936-1940 which finally broke them.

In between these years they dealt with mouse plagues more than once. The only means they had to reduce their numbers was a bath filled with water. A bait in a bottle was placed in the middle for the mice to crawl out to, fall in and drown. It wasn't an effective system to combat the thousands upon thousands and speaks to their inability in the end to overcome and thrive with all that was thrown at them.

Roy's sister's husband, Archie, who had a little more capital behind him was able to weather the conditions and increase his property to

5000 acres, largely by buying up some of the Closer and Settlement Schemes land when people walked off their properties. 5000 acres plus is a viable farm in the Mallee.

Roy and Nell's oldest two sons had left school at the end of Grade Six. Schools were largely seen as a burden by families in the district.

Even with the boys help and the assistance of neighbours working together they were on a hiding to nowhere. Both of these boys became excellent horsemen with one becoming a drover travelling up through Queensland and working the Queensland rodeo circuit for a few years.

After riding the 2,200km back to Victoria, he enlisted in the army with the hope of joining the occupational forces in Japan post W.W.2. That ride was to be a saddle sore warm up for a ride across the country to Perth.

Two years in the army got him as far as Melbourne. He picked up a mate in the forces and in 1948 they set out for the West Coast.

They didn't chase work. It was all about the journey.

Perth and back is only a 6,600km return trip. Just down the road, really.

The journey was definitely somewhere in the league of Nedd Brockmann who in 2022 did a Forest Gump and ran from Perth to Sydney. For them that was only half way. They had to saddle up and make the return trip.

Sadly, his mate committed suicide not long after their return to Victoria. He became another ex-soldier statistic.

My uncle, sticking with his horse, found work taking supplies on packhorse from Bright to the ski lodges on the surrounding mountains, for the next two years.

What a different world Victorias ski industry was in 1950.

At the beginning of the '40s time had come for the family to leave the clear night skies of the Mallee and make a different life elsewhere. Looking to a more settled area of the state they choose the Western District.

In their thirteen years at Karween the house was only lit by candles, lanterns or kerosine lights. When eventually they bought a Tilley lamp no-one could believe how bright the night could be lit up. They even attached it to the front of the Model-T Ford to go to the Saturday night dances.

When you consider the marketing around clear night skies as a tourism drawcard today, I can't help but think that for them the dark enclosing night was just another aspect of their isolation however beautiful they might have deemed it.

In 1940 Roy and his oldest son, who was now 16, put their pushbikes on the train in Mildura and, travelling via Melbourne, disembarked in Colac. Then they rode to Alvie to check out a dairy share farm in the heart of a region known for its volcanic craters. The property carried 80 cows and their income was a percentage of the milk sales.

Roy had surprised himself because in their time in the Mallee he had ranked dairying almost last on a list of farming options.

After agreeing to the deal and with no money in their pockets, they rode their bikes back to Karween.

Riding 650kms on crappy 1930's bikes on crappy 1940s gravel roads and tracks is an incomparable challenge to riding that distance today. Sleeping on the ground beside the road each night simply added to the joy of aching bodies.

Now it was time to sell, and sell everything to generate some cash for kickstarting a new life.

The 500 acres, with improvements, was handed back to the government. The Victorian government re-bundled the 500 acre lots into 5000 acres and on-sold them.

Livestock, farm equipment and thirteen years of collected odds and sods you find in a farmer's shed or farmhouse were sold. Even tines and horseshoes went. The clearance sale realised 400 pounds, but there was an outstanding grocery bill.

Roy bought a 1928 Austin Six for the trip south and all eight said goodbye to the light sandy soil of the Mallee with the hope the rich volcanic soil west of Colac offered a different life.

Everyone was jammed into the Austin with nothing but the clothes on their back.

There was no bedding, no kitchen items, nothing but the family. Everything, their whole way of life, was gone.

Travelling night and day was necessary when you have eight people jammed into an old Austin.

The oldest son came kicking and screaming.

At 16 he had been out of school four years working the farm and knew only a life the Mallee provided.

Change is often hardest for those starting to make their own way in life, in a world they are only just beginning to get a handle on.

One newspaper of the time described the northwest corner of Victoria as 'a Sahara of hissing hot winds and red driving sand, a carrion polluted wilderness'.

True, if a little dramatic.

Nevertheless, it was home to many families in the decades between the wars.

Adjusting to the cold and wet of the Western District meant getting shoes and for some of the boys this was a first.

After one year in the share dairy farm they were still broke.

The solution was to plant out 30 acres in Spanish brown onions, which they continued to do for four years. The onions boosted their finances but once again the size of the property could not return a reasonable income.

Whilst in Alvie, Roy's father, John, (of course) came to live with them. His doctor diagnosed heart problems and suggested he not live on his own. It was a spectacularly incorrect diagnosis as he lived with them for 20 years, dying at the age of 92.

Nell and Roy had over twenty years of farming behind them but nothing in the bank account to show for it. Moving off land and living in town was the sensible next step.

In the non-indigenous history of Australia being rural poor has always seemed better than being city poor. Maybe a romanticised element comes into play here. After all, you are in the Great Outdoors of Australia, having a go and trying to make something of your life for yourself and future generations.

Being city poor carries stronger images of deprivation and loss of dignity. The romance is lacking.

At the end of the day poor is poor but if you are not 'idle poor' and you 'owe no man anything', people can still carry their dignity.

The family left farming poor but with their dignity. They simply got a poor (sorry for the bad pun) return on their labour.

Not quite being able to move to a suburban block, Roy negotiated the purchase of three acres, and an unliveable house, in Elliminyt on the edge of Colac. It was a handshake deal requiring regular payments. The house was made liveable and it became home till Roy's death.

The original owner died and his two sons continued the handshake deal until the property was owned outright.

Imagine how many upset lawyers we would have in Australia if two people could make a handshake deal and stick to it because the word of both parties was enough to make it happen.

1946 ticked over and Roy had work in an onion dehydration factory whilst doing the early morning milk round. People would leave empty milk bottles on their doorstep with the money for that day's milk. Clearly coin theft wasn't a significant issue even when the people around you are poor.

His next job was with State Rivers and Water Supply. For two years he worked in and around Birregurra. His Mallee experience came in handy.

This was the first time they had money in their pockets but Roy could only afford to come home for the weekend, fuel prices being what they were in the years after WW2.

His mode of transport was a 1938 AJS motorbike and Birregurra was only 20kms from home, but still... there was a tyranny of distance or perhaps more accurately a tyranny of the cost of living.

Roy, about to hit his fifth decade, commenced lay preaching at the end of the 1940s for the Presbyterian Church, in the back blocks of the Otway Ranges. He was semi regular at Lavers Hill and Carlisle River.

1948 rang in another work change, blacksmithing for Colac Shire. Roy remained a blacksmith until retirement in 1966. Work involved sharpening horse scoops, picks and shovels, making grader tines, working on pneumatic drills and other day to day tasks such as being the surveyor's assistant.

The 1938 AJS became a '49 AJS 350 and, finally, a '28 Chevrolet Tourer making it easier for them to get around together. Nell became the children's story teller when Roy preached.

Despite experiencing hard years in the Mallee, the Mallee never left their blood.

In retirement they often drove back to the region that was such a formative part of their life. Everything was so alive for them in those years of battling plagues, falling crop prices, drought and the Great Depression.

> Were they 'fit as a mallee bull' and 'tough as a mallee root' through those years? (The reader can decide.)

The soil, the climate, the lessons in life had become an intrinsic part of who they were. Faith, hope and love carried them through, and it was a faith, hope and love partly fashioned by the Mallee. Geography had etched its own lines on their bodies and in their souls.

Roy died in 1973 after battling diabetes from his middle thirties on.

They never had a home with space just to themselves. Not only did John live with them for 20 years but Nell's parents spent their last three years with them as did an aunt of Roys', whose sons, while farming near Birregurra, couldn't look after her anymore.

Their house was an open door for family with nowhere to go.

Nell lived on dying at 93 in 1993.

And so, one branch of the fourth-generation of our people came and went contributing to the welfare of their family and community, living a very Australian life in starkly diverse parts of Victoria.

Other branches of the fourth generation who successfully made a life on the land built up a substantial property in the Mallee or productive cattle properties in the Western District of Victoria.

Roy's brothers' youngest son dominated A.F.L. football in the Hampton League and at the beginning of the 1950s was drafted to a Melbourne club to play in what was then arguably the elite level of A.F.L., the Victorian Football League. He was over 6ft., mobile, had a big engine and was built like a brick dunny. These are highly desirable traits in a contact sport.

Football being an amateur sport provided no genuine livelihood in the 50s. He played one season but was unhappy with the whole 'package' sport offered, especially the living in Melbourne aspect. He returned to the Western District to work the farm, serve on the local council and play football.

Later in life he became a minister and somewhat ironically served in a church in Melbourne and then Perth.

You can hardly talk about Australian lives without the subject of sport coming up in some form and so I note here that in the seventh generation, our daughter, at the age of 15 was chased by Vic Netball to play in the Under 16 Victorian team. She played goal attack.

Vic Netball kept asking because her skills were state level but our daughter kept hanging back. She balked at playing in Melbourne, at the level of intensity required to play for your state. At 15 she was a walk in but she was only 15 so her final decision, and right decision, was to continue playing locally.

These two stories, separated by two generations, speak to where the majority of Australians engage in sport. When a sport stops being fun, when it stops giving back to you as much as you put into it, we disengage.

The enjoyment spectrum is just as relevant to the least athletic of us through to professionals.

Sport changed significantly in two generations but the clear conclusion for both was sport has to be fun.

CHAPTER THREE

Now it's time to leave those who carry my surname and draw a couple of brief sketches on my mother's side, so let's get the freaky-deaky stuff out of the way first because we do not leave my father's people completely.

My great grandmother, Alice, who had arrived in Australia from Scotland in 1887, married at 19 and had my grandmother, Alice. She died two weeks after the birth from complications, an all-too-common story for the times.

It still astounds me how life can throw you such great moments of joy and elation and then take your breath away with tragedy.

Alice was raised by a step mum, Annie, and her father Henry, who married one year after her mother died. They had five more children together. Annie had second cousins, Jemina and Helen, who married brothers John (of course) and James (a moniker which has almost caught up with the Johns now) blankety-blank my surname.

Freaky-deaky!

My parents were oblivious to this connection two generations before them when they got together.

My mother's side were Barwon Heads people and Connewarre where the first John and family settled is 20 kms away. Consequently, it is not surprising some members of both families, who remained in the area, would cross socially two generations on.

Barwon Heads, at the mouth of the Barwon River, got its European migrant start with a small fishing fleet which berthed in the river. Beautiful timbered barracoota boats were put to sail and fished not far from the Barwon Heads Bluff. Prior to this the Bluff area was an important food source for the Wathaurong people too.

In 1910 Henry and Annie opened the first bakery in Barwon Heads. It was such an event that a social and dance night was held in the Barwon Heads Recreation Hall on Monday October 3. Fancy costumes, comedic renditions of songs, recitations and playing cards were part of the proceeding. Supper, at midnight, catered for 150 people. Just about the whole of the town must have crammed into the hall.

Dancing started after supper and went to the early hours of morning. Quite the event.

Did they all have Tuesday off?

The couple operated the bakery together and, much later the family opened a bakery in Lorne too.

Having working parents meant baby Alice was usually left outside the bakery in her pram, with their dalmatian. Customers would chat to baby and dog, buy their bread etc and continue on not thinking anything unusual had transpired.

An everyday event surely.

So, when did leaving a pram outside a shop, perhaps when you were grabbing a couple of basic needs, cease? Why did it cease?

Perhaps the majority of us missed one of the great social indicators of a change in Australian society involving parental responsibilities, mental health issues in the community, crime, small town confidence in those we call neighbours, social expectations and more.

Babies. Prams. Shops. Mmmm.

In 1926-27 Henry worked on the construction of the Barwon Heads Bridge near the mouth of the river. Prior to this you could only get to Ocean Grove by boat as the river was an inaccessible barrier.

The bridge became the longest surviving timber stringer road bridge in Victoria for some years before reconstruction in 2009. It quite often featured as a backdrop on the popular Australian television program Seachange, filmed in and around Barwon Heads, which ran for three seasons at the end of the nineties.

The revamped bridge and a walk bridge built beside it in 2009 were somewhat controversial. A group of locals, especially some Barwon Heads business people, pushed for the bridge to remain in the same location at the mouth of the Barwon River.

Population growth, and common sense, should have dictated the bridge be built further down the river to enable a smoother flow of traffic through Barwon Heads. The bridges' location now has the potential, too often realised, to create the worst traffic jams on The Bellarine.

If only this had happened nine years earlier Seachange could have had another plotline for an episode or two on our TVs.

Henry diversified his working interests. He also had a silver mine at Steiglitz out the other side of Geelong. You had to find a dollar, or pound, where you could in the 1920s and 1930s.

Alice would leave behind her pram, grow up, marry Ted, and have one daughter, Alice. Yes, they were just as imaginative with their names as the other mob.

Ted had been a latchkey kid. Both parents died before he was 10 and he was handed around relatives, none of who really wanted another mouth to feed.

He worked hand-to-mouth jobs, loved trotting and cards, and had a sizeable vegie patch.

Later, as part of their income, Ted and 'Alice the Second' owned a corner milk bar with Ted also working for International Harvester.

Even in the 1950s and early 60s large biscuit tins lined the shelves, and the décor of their shop was largely timber. Customers bought biscuits, weighed on their scales, in brown paper bags for them to take home. Cold Coke, in summer, was sold by the glass. Cricketers, who played on the oval in front of their milk bar, spent their break sitting under their veranda drinking Coke before bowling a few more overs.

The third and final Alice, my mother, like most in her generation, left school at the end of Year 8. She worked mostly in factories until marrying when 26.

In wrapping up this brief diversion to my mother's people I venture back to the freaky.

When Alice the Third was around 20 an American dentist came to Geelong pitching the line 'now is the time to get false teeth'. He offered a great price. Why wait?

My mother and her girlfriends were all single and had worked for some years. Some, like my mother, worked at Collins Bros, a woollen mill that made blankets. Situated on the Barwon River, near Landy Field, Geelong's current athletic track, the firm was also known for its lit signage illuminating the night, something of a rarity in the post-W.W.2 decade.

The women could afford to have their teeth pulled whereas after marriage the opportunity might not present.

Such was their logic and such were the times.

In they marched to the dentist, plonked themselves in his chair, and promptly had all their teeth pulled. A wonderful set of sparkling falsies were fitted and everyone was happy. There were many who took up this amazing offer.

Wow! Wow! Wow!

Expectations were so different eight decades ago that no-one thought the dentist was a shyster. The dentist would not have even thought he was taking people for a ride. This was a good business making a genuine offer.

Good one, Alice.

CHAPTER FOUR

And so, we come to us... but not yet.

There is still my wife's people and they definitely have a tale. They came from another part of over yonder a century after my mob.

1954 to be exact.

Why did they set their eyes on Australia?

There were no severe food shortages. There were no massed forced evictions from the land; or, to talk in terms of their 1950s economy, there were no great shutdowns in business nor plummeting fortunes after W.W.2.

Growing opportunities for work, for education, for better incomes, were part and parcel of their country's post war surge. Although, in this context, it should be noted the family's second business was not as successful as their first.

Unlike John and Janet adventure was their principal motivation, albeit there were different perspectives across the family on what was deemed an adventure.

Oskar had always wanted to see the world but was prevented from travelling by the pressing need to help provide for his younger siblings. Then came marriage and a family that grew to six children.

His itch still needed scratching and a sort of consensus to leave village life and embark on a different course for the rest of their lives in the far flung reaches of the Southern Hemisphere was reached.

Similarities between the first-generation Australians in each family are freakish. Both sets of parents were in the first half of their forties when they arrived and each family had six kids whose ages were almost identical, ranging from 20 to 5. John's family were joiners and stonemasons. Oskar was a joiner.

When they first put feet on Australian soil the family consisted of: Oskar (44), Gertrude (42), Margrit (20), Susan (18), Oskar (16), Theodor (15), Walter (13) and Regina (4).

So why was 1953/54 a good time to leave Switzerland?

The family came through the war years living in a small village called Mannedorf on Lake Zurich, 20kms from Zurich. At least the family had.

Oskar spent the whole of the war, six years, as a guard on Switzerland's borders.

Occasionally he got leave and occasionally Gertrude (Trudi) could go to see him but no-one was to know where he was stationed.

If the church bells rang, when the men were on leave, they had to immediately don their uniforms and head for the train station.

During the war years Trudi turned her hand to making and selling grave clothes, a somewhat grim income, to help the family survive financially.

School could be irregular as teachers also did short stints on the borders. Soldiers would sleep in their classrooms, on straw, and Trudi's business was also used for bedding at night.

A positive for the family was the soldiers made food in big vats and they were able to collect some in a saucepan.

They never went hungry.

Home grown vegetables were stored for the winter months and in autumn they took their handcart to nearby farmers to buy up apples and potatoes in bulk to also store in their cellar. Maize based meals were common. The maize came from a plot they rented. Each Saturday they could get bread from the bakery and in spring family walks in the forest involved foraging for wild fruits.

Then it was back to their blacked out home and semi-normal life. The day the war ended the children were collecting empty toothpaste tubes for the lead and the village church bells rang to the tune of realised hope.

It was a 'where were you' when something dramatic transpires in life. They knew exactly where they were and what they were doing.

Relief burst from them in pure joy.

When we think of Switzerland being neutral in WW2 it is easy to picture war raging around them while the country remained a mountain retreat for peace.

Surely the hills were alive only with 'The Sound of Music'.

Not so.

Switzerland's war was one of armed neutrality which in reality involved walking a precarious tightrope.

Throughout the war German planes flew over their home at night on bombing raids. On one occasion bombs were dropped over the hill from Mannedorf. The sound of bombs exploding stayed with them and consequently the Avalon Airshow dredges up memories.

They also remembered women standing at the end of their village crying for lost ones. Some came to Trudi for grave clothes.

Oskar was part of the initial mobilisation of 430,000 combat troops. Over the war this number grew to 850,000.

In the early stages of the war Germany developed a plan to invade Switzerland, a plan never realised.

By wars end 33 Swiss spies for Nazi Germany had been sentenced to death and a further 99 found guilty of treason and undermining Swiss neutrality.

From enemies within to enemies on the border the Swiss were kept busy. Germany repeatedly violated Swiss airspace. In 1940 the Swiss shot down 11 German planes and the Germans shot down three of theirs. The ensuing policy change was to force German planes to land on Swiss airfields.

Later Germany sent saboteurs to destroy those airfields.

The Swiss captured them.

Skirmishes along Switzerland's northern border continued throughout the war.

Oskar was stationed in the north and he definitely didn't spend his time cleaning his rifle, admiring the view, playing his alpenhorn and yodelling.

Racial minorities and other groups of people were continually trying to flee war across the Swiss border. The Swiss fearing Hitler's response if they maintained an open border policy placed approximately 300,000 refugees in border camps.

This was Oskar's front yard for the war.

The Swiss also built up a substantial armoury through fear the Axis powers would ignore their neutral stance. Most of this weaponry was destroyed at the end of W.W.2.

It wasn't only the Germans who violated Swiss airspace. As war progressed Allied pilots would also violate their airspace. These violations were partly motivated by the logic, especially when low on fuel, it is better to face internment in Switzerland than potentially becoming a P.O.W. elsewhere.

The Swiss, walking that tightrope of neutrality, grounded 100 planes and interned their crews, some of who tried to escape to France.

As late as 1944 there were 160 American airmen retained in the Swiss prison camp at Wauwilermoos.

Others not so fortunate died as the Swiss fought to maintain neutrality.

One of Switzerland's more notable and beautiful tourist towns, Schaffhausen, was accidentally bombed by the Americans in 1944.

44 people were killed.

After the Schaffhausen incident the Swiss adopted a zero tolerance for Allied and Axis planes in their airspace.

Consequently, a period of confusion in the air occurred and a number of Axis, Allied and Swiss planes were shot down.

Then the Americans 'accidentally' bombed Basel and Zurich.

These incidents appear to have been a tit-for-tat knee-jerk response to Switzerland's armed neutrality policy over their airspace.

Oskar did a stint guarding a bridge in Zurich but whether the timing coincided with the bombing is unknown. Swiss official secrets... yarda-yarda.

At wars end Oskar came home and the family went about rebuilding their lives and their joinery business. Neither was easy. Prolonged absences require a knitting back together in relationships and confidence has to be rebuilt in business.

The war had stolen a father for six years.

Unlike most Swiss who have long term lease arrangements for housing, Oskar returned to his house in Mannedorf.

His joinery workshop and business were located beside their home and for as long as they had this business Oskar employed one or two joiners to work for him. One boarded with them during the week and returned home on weekends and the other boarded in the village.

The difficulties of travel being what they were saw Roy doing the same thing in Birregurra, Australia, at a similar time.

Oskar's workshop was versatile making everything from standard joinery jobs to window construction to producing furniture but it was time to make a move.

The business was sold and the family moved to a neighbouring village, Staffa. The move gave Oskar an opportunity to build his own house. Getting into building alongside joinery and furniture making was something he wanted to do.

While construction was happening, the family moved to a holiday house in the mountains. During this time the oldest daughter, Margrit, having left school at 14, was doing the book work for the business and attending commercial school at night.

The business they established in Staffa was not as successful as Mannedorf, partly because, somewhat bizarrely, they were seen as foreigners by some villagers.

Five minutes further down Lake Zurich, by car, made you a foreigner.

What a small-world early 1950s Switzerland could be.

Building the house and relocating the business was not enough to satisfy Oskar's itch. He began to look beyond Switzerland again.

Oskar's first choice was Canada but Trudi refused to go to another country just as cold as Switzerland. As she could speak French, she wanted to go only as far as the French speaking part of Switzerland. Oskar could only speak Swiss-German. He did not want to learn French and besides he was looking to the world.

South Africa had come into discussions but in the end, they settled on Australia as the best option for the family as a whole. Trudi and Oskar started to attend English classes at night.

It was decided Oskar would come to Australia first, earn some coin, and start to get established in readiness for the family. He had also learnt that to get the Australian pension you had to be in the workforce for at least 20 years. This was an added motivation to get Down Under and get started on a new life.

In August 1953 he set sail from Naples after travelling by train from Switzerland with Margrit, who was the family send-off rep. He landed in Melbourne and came to Geelong because of a Swiss man he met.

Oscar's first job was building Commission Homes which were basically kit-homes shipped in from France.

As he worked in Geelong the family sold up everything and prepared for the move.

It was through this transition phase that Walter, the fifth child, started his unenviable record of doing Grade 6 three times. Two attempts were made in the German speaking part of Switzerland as their education was broken up with time spent boarding in the Italian speaking part of Switzerland while the house and business in Staffa were sold. The third was in Australia.

While they were in the southeast of Switzerland, where the Swiss speak Italian, the boys were left to their own devices. They loved the freedom of hiking and climbing in the local mountains. On one occasion their reckless nature got the best of them. Looking over a cliff they spotted an eagle's nest not too far down. They decided to jump down to it not knowing whether the nest would hold one young teenage boy let alone two.

Theodor (Teddy) and Walter survived the challenge, without an eagle coming at them, and climbed back up.

Christmas 1953 was their last Christmas in Switzerland. For Swiss the whole Santa thing happens on December 6. Christmas trees decorated on Christmas Eve, candles, family time and hot food on a cold winter's day was what Christmas Day was all about.

Christmas was never quite the same in Australia no matter how Australian they became. Hot food on a hot day?? Nah.

As things were being sorted Oskar wrote a proforma letter to the family requiring each of the children to indicate whether they were coming to Australia or not. In a nod to Swiss democracy this was their final casting vote.

Remember the older children were in the workforce and beginning to make their own way in life, and Regina was only 4.

The boys enthusiastically voted yes. For them they were embarking on another big adventure.

The two oldest girls wrote ditto underneath.

They were very reluctant but because the family expectation was you contributed to the family's well-being until you reached 20, they wrote 'ditto'.

Margrit had had five years out of school, completed a business certificate course, was working in an office for a firm that sold and installed ventilation systems, had had stints away from the family, boarding, had supported the family financially when Trudi was ill, and had a boy quite keen on her.

Her life was not pointing towards Australia.

Susan was also working, at a telephone exchange, had supported the family financially and had been accepted into a fine arts school. Her life was not across the Equator.

Ditto. Ditto.

All seven came.

The girls' story is the same as Roy's oldest son, who struggled to leave the Mallee, but family required some giving back before you could fully own your own life.

Waving goodbye they boarded the train. Aunts, uncles, brothers, sisters, all believed they would never see Trudi and family again in this life.

A Swiss man, who had worked on P & O Liners and knew English, assisted them. He sorted labels for their luggage as words like cabin and hold were foreign. Travelling with them by train to Naples, he warded off Italian beggars and spoke to the crew of Oronsay to get them aboard.

There was some confusion because a woman with six children in tow did not generally travel First Class.

Tourist Class. Yes. First Class. No.

After a whole lot of apologising, they were welcomed on ship. The girls thought the whole clumsy affair was hilarious.

They had saved every franc to make First Class possible. The joinery business fetched an acceptable price and Oskar had sent some money.

He kept his equipment because it was familiar and the latest. Oskar also knew if you travel First Class you can take as much weight in cargo as you wanted. It was a motivating factor in purchasing those tickets. Everything from chisels to G-clamps to lathes came to Australia.

Nine months after Oskar landed on these shores the family set sail on the Oronsay in 1954.

The Oronsay, built in 1948 and named after the Isle of Oron on Scotland's west coast, had seven decks for First Class, with comfortable post-war cabins and silver service. It could carry 1551 passengers with 668 in First Class.

In contrast 102 years earlier, John and family sailed in steerage in cramped conditions where you often lacked fresh air and had to provide your own bed and food.

But I wonder if people would have been so keen to board the Oronsay if they knew it caught fire in the final stages of construction. So much water was poured into the hold to quell the fire that the ship listed 20 degrees. In danger of sinking, the experts decided to cut a large hole in the hull to release water.

After this ominous start Oronsay was launched in 1950. The vessel proved to be safe and reliable in its 25 years of cruising, although there was an incident between Melbourne and Sydney after the family disembarked.

The Oronsay was to carry the one millionth post W.W.2 migrant to Australia in 1955, the year after their voyage.

On their voyage the majority of the passengers boarded in England and were on an around the world trip. It was early days in the rebirthing of cruising post W.W.2.

They had smooth sailing from Naples to the Suez Canal, their first stop. Egyptian police came on board asking for cigarettes only to be frustrated as they had none.

Seriously, what sort of First-Class passengers were they?

The world dramatically changed before their eyes as they sailed the Canal. Ships ran at about seven knots through the Suez so they had a passing vista of camels, palm trees and miles of desert. The world before their eyes stretched their imagination.

Second stop was Aden, in Yemen. Aden was still a British colony in 1954. The British originally took control of Aden in 1839 to better protect their shipping coming out of British India.

Today, Aden is best known for piracy and extremism. Their old ways of 180 years ago have returned.

Aden, in 1954, had been in a drought for years, but it wasn't on land that the most notable event occurred when they were there.

An aircraft carrier was anchored near the Oronsay. This was protection for Queen Elizabeth who sailed through on the Britannia at 1am that night. Not knowing who she was they still figured she must be some big deal to have an aircraft carrier standing guard. They watched with curiosity.

Colombo, Sri Lanka, was the next port.

Colombo sowed some serious doubts in the minds of the family. (It should be noted Trudi was ill on the boat and the kids were on their own in town, as they were for the entire trip.) They were shocked by the conditions witnessed in the city.

Beggars pursued them and the crowds jostled and pushed their way down streets and in shops. Australia was a huge mistake if it was anything like Colombo.

Safely back on-board the Oronsay they were still dismayed by passengers throwing coins into the sea for boys to dive and collect. People being reduced to begging sickened them and they were keen to leave the stench of Colombo behind.

Onward sailed Oronsay into the baby blue Indian Ocean.

The weather quickly changed and soon they were crashing though big swells. The Oronsay would rise on the first wave, glide into the second, rise higher again, then carve though the third wave spilling the oceans' turbulence across the deck. From your cabin window you would see nothing but sea then nothing but sky.

For two days the Indian Ocean dished up its worst.

The children, aged 20 to 4, were on their own again.

Essentially, Trudi had a nervous breakdown on the ship. A reluctance to leave Switzerland, the stress of closing up their affairs, the family split into different locations while she managed the final details of moving and her trepidation for what now lay ahead, caught up with her.

It was left to the older girls and the ship stewards to keep an eye on them.

They sampled all sorts of foreign foods and pursued the ice-cream man when he came around. Salted butter was just plain wrong. They swam in the pool at night after everyone was in bed and choked initially on the salt water, something they had never come across.

Risky behaviour re-emerged with the boys. Growing up with iced lakes and snow it wasn't a great leap in the boy's imagination to ski down the outside steps, when they were wet from the swell with the roll of the boat. Great fun until Walter slipped and ended up balancing on the outer rail of the ship staring a long way down into the ocean's gaping mouth.

The fun ended.

The sea calmed again and they safely anchored at Fremantle, a little off-shore. A pilot boat, with customs on-board, came out to the ship. When they had the all clear they went ashore again, minus Trudi.

This was not Colombo.

Phew, as in relief, not phew, as in disgusting stench!

While the houses were completely foreign, they were nothing like what was seen on the journey out. People looked healthy and seemed to live life similar to what they knew. Parks and public places were lovely and they witnessed their first cricket match. The boys lumped cricket in the bizarre and stupid category.

Things would change.

For the final leg of their voyage, they had to embrace the Southern Ocean on their way to Port Adelaide and Melbourne.

It was rough, rough, rough.

Port Adelaide was industrial with no housing and this was where for the first time in their lives they experienced walking on dry grass.

As INXS said 'a new sensation'.

Onward to Victoria.

A pilot boat from Queenscliff came out to meet them outside the Heads to Port Phillip Bay.

All hail the pilot who, that day, had to climb the ladder in unfriendly seas to come aboard and steer Oronsay safely into the Bay.

Cruising up Port Phillip they noticed the beach huts on the foreshore of the Mornington Peninsula and commented, 'I am not going to live in one of those little boxes'.

Now they would love to own one if only for its real estate value.

The ship, due on May 11, docked one day early at Station Pier.

There was no way to inform Oskar they had arrived so the crew allowed them to spend the night on board and enjoy one last First Class meal.

The following day two cars pulled up at the pier. Oskar had made friends. He could not drive, and as the years passed that did not change. He never owned a car.

All seven were standing on the pier waiting with their luggage piled up beside them. A customs man began to slowly check through their property but when one of Oskar's friends handed him a ten pound note they were cleared instantly.

The Oronsay sailed on but between Melbourne and Sydney it lost its stabilisers after having dealt with one too many violent seas on this trip.

With everyone and everything jammed into the cars, they set off for Geelong. All of Oskar's workshop machinery and tools were delivered by courier at a later date.

This was the road to a new world for them. Barbed wire in the Melbourne port area and barbed wire on fences along the Geelong Road had them wondering what sort of country they had come to. Barbed wire had very different connotations for them with their recent memories of W.W.2.

Drivers stuck their hand out the window to indicate when turning right or left.

These people are a 'Weird Mob'.

In 1954 the Geelong-Melbourne Road was a bituminised single lane. You had to get off in the gravel to let a car coming the other way pass. It is now the busiest road in Australia ranging between six and eight lanes.

No-one in the family had ever been in a car, public transport being what it was in Switzerland.

It was exhilarating and daunting.

For them the country was unbelievably flat and endless.

Slowly driving past the You Yangs they wondered if those pimples were as big as mountains got in Australia.

In the nine months Oskar had been here he built prefab houses for the growing number of workers in Geelong's manufacturing industries. Shell, Ford, International Harvester and other manufacturers were expanding. Many of the new workers were European migrants.

Oskar had met another Swiss Australian who had recently bought a run-down house in East Geelong. This was their first Australian home.

Once again, they were left wondering about what they left behind.

Their Swiss home had an automatic washing machine, a fridge, central heating, an inside toilet, a swimming pool, and was sealed up against winter weather.

The old weatherboard house had none of the above and offered an icebox for a fridge and a copper for boiling clothes to wash.

The house once had character but that was now questionable. The garden and yard were a wilderness.

They were grateful for a roof over their heads, a bed to sleep in and a starting point for a new life.

Their Australian adventure was under way and as soon as Myers received an expected shipment of white goods, Trudi made sure her name was at the top of the list for a refrigerator.

Unfortunately, Trudis' breakdown, which began on the Oronsay, was to continue for some time.

Where to for their first meal in Australia?

A friend who could translate for them directed them to a pub.

Welcome to Australia.

The most discussed menu item that night was jelly for dessert. How can you eat something which only wants to bounce and go in all directions? And as for the texture in your mouth??

The language barrier created frustrating situations for them but it also provided amusing moments. On one occasion Margrit and Susan were buying dress fabric in Myers. They asked the sales assistant for fabric with 'full stops' on it.

Out of the ensuing confusion they were finally able to bring home some polka-dot fabric to make a dress. They would take a dictionary with them when shopping and could not comprehend why the sales woman did not understand their improving English.

In no time the oldest four children were working and the girls were boarding away from home, in Geelong.

Work was also under way with their house in Herne Hill, another suburb of Geelong.

The family began to attend a Presbyterian church because they heard Swiss reformers had influenced the founding of Presbyterianism. Their early months simply involved following the actions of others and noting the end came with a chorus of 'amen'.

There was a sense of God being in the place even though they had static on their line to Him and to others.

Margrit worked as a kitchenhand at Morongo Girls School which was a Presbyterian private school for the fairly well off in Geelong and the Western District. A number of women lived there because of the high number of students who boarded. Their day commenced with 7am breakfast.

Mixing with everyday Australians gave her the opportunity to improve her language skills. After tea the women had informal English classes for the migrant workers. There were other Europeans employed by the school. Being Geelong, the discussions often revolved around football (A.F.L.).

Team sports were foreign to Margrit and she was stunned everyone here seemed to be involved in sport on some level.

I am sure she learnt important stuff like, that's a mark, go long, just kick the damn thing, shanked it, handball it, shepherd him, shepherd, speccie or screamer, attack the ball and tackle him don't bump.

With her little English she applied for an office job at Myers and was employed because she had good references and Swiss qualifications. The typewriters and other office machines proved to be antique compared to what she had worked with in Switzerland.

Working the phone was the most challenging aspect of the job, especially getting people's names right.

One of her bosses called her a Red Indian because of her language. Hearing this I was amused as travelling through Oklahoma and Texas with my wife we had kids point and say; 'look mum an Indian'. Like mother, like daughter.

It might have had something to do with olive skin and plaited black hair.

On the home front the owner of their East Geelong rental wanted to sell off the house's contents. What ensued was a bewildering and frightening day where people poured through buying up everything including carpets which were pulled up, and plants, ripped from the garden.

Their few possessions were stacked in one room they stood guard on.

School commenced for the youngest two.

Walter had his third shot at Grade 6 and Regina began her school life. She was very reluctant to attend. Her only exposure to English was the trip to Australia.

In her first few days she found it difficult communicating but then she came home and said to her mother; 'School is okay. They all speak Swiss'.

Obviously, the reverse was true. She had picked up so much English so quickly that she thought everyone could speak Swiss.

Regina is a classic example of a child's ability to communicate and acquire language through play, and learning to 'read' another person's meaning and intent. Linguistic experts believe age 0-6 is the critical stage in a child's ability to shape and expand their language.

The phase when all children, irrespective of their language and culture, learn similar words from the same categories is referred to as Universal Grammar.

Playing with English speaking children aboard the Oronsay informally taught Regina sounds, objects, actions, vocabulary and the structure of English at its most fundamental and critical level. Imitation and repetition reinforce the brain's amazing capabilities at this age.

Nouns and verbs associated with a noun are the starting point for language and with the free flow of language between children, the freedom to make mistakes without fear of error, age 0-6 remains a unique stage in a person's life.

From our seventh year on the brain loses its ability to absorb and shape language in the same free flowing manner and language becomes more of a case of you have to study to learn.

For Walter, English held him back while Maths, the universal language, was a breeze.

In the 1950s E.S.L. (English as a Second Language) consisted of listening, and hopefully interpreting and understanding, some of the classroom discourse. If you had a teacher with some German, French or Italian, languages Walter was more familiar with, the teacher might say something like 'le porte' and the French kid would go to the door. That was as good as an E.S.L. lesson got.

Inevitably, with his disjointed schooling, he left at the end of Year 8, when he was 16, and commenced working for his father building furniture, shelving, doors etc.

Later, in his 20s, he completed a degree at Melbourne University.

It was around this time Susan ended up in hospital twice.

On the first occasion she walked through long grass from Eastern Beach to East Geelong. The following day her legs were swollen and covered in blisters.

What sort of country was this where not only are the animals hazardous but so is 'the grass'?

Australia was a different beast to Switzerland. As a younger girl she could play Heidi and skip through alpine wildflower meadows.

Here you watched where you walk, for multiple reasons.

The second hospital visit was for what tends to be a European Mediterranean problem; hair follicles growing inwardly at the base of the back. Untreated they can grow centimetres long and are very painful.

This was her second operation, the first being in Switzerland, which was botched.

The Swiss doctor knew the operation was not a success and even volunteered to waiver his bill.

Different times.

She spent several weeks on the hospitals terrace in June/July of 1955. There were no windows, only canvas blinds to cover the openings. Biting southwesters curved in off Bass Strait with whispers of Antarctica.

It was a penetrating cold quite unlike the still chill of Switzerland.

1950s Australian medical care could be conducted under a veranda and only a migrant would think it odd.

It was an eye-opening experience.

As soon as their house had two complete rooms the family moved in, a common story in the fifties. Being able to get into your house this quick prevented lost time in trying to save for a substantial deposit and lost money gone to renting.

The first small supermarkets appeared in Geelong making a huge difference to migrant's weekly shops. Self-serve, being able to walk around and find what you wanted, simplified what had been an arduous task. No more pointing and stumbling through the German-English dictionary for the right words.

In the early fifties there was a delicatessen in Geelong where all the migrants put their name on a list for when the next boat came in bearing coffee. The standard coffee substitute Australians drank was a liquid chickory essence, a vile comparison for European coffee taste buds.

The family got used to butcher's shops with big chunks of meat hanging from butcher's hooks. Initially our humble butchers were quite a shock to the eye.

Not a single schnitzel could be seen anywhere in 1954.

Meanwhile, oldest daughter Margrit, after being in Australia 18 months, was growing restless. In late '55 she bought a return ticket to Switzerland and set sail.

At least she could speak English on the boat this time.

She had maintained correspondence with a bloke in Switzerland but her principal reason for leaving was to find her own way in the world.

She felt she could not be fully independent in Australia.

Australia hadn't been her dream.

After experiencing one Australian summer, and being badly sunburnt, she longed for all things Swiss, especially a white Christmas.

Margrit went back to her office job with the ventilation firm in Zurich. She had been corresponding with them also.

The relationship with the boyfriend imploded. It was never going anywhere despite the early phase, pre-Australia, when she would climb out her bedroom window and visit him.

Soon it became clear the independence she sought was not to be found in Switzerland. She was a different woman.

Australia had changed her.

Swiss skies now loomed overhead. People were nosier. The odd nosey relative still wanted to tell her the workforce was not for women.

Margrit didn't feel she had the same freedom to go where she wanted and do what she wanted. Village life was village life. The Swiss, overall, weren't as openly friendly as Australians nor as carefree.

Vestiges of Australia clung to her, were her.

She met Alfred (Fred) at work. Six months later an office romance began. Fred was into skiing and had already travelled across Europe and Great Britain. Margrit would talk to him about Australia, about its' vastness, its' big skies and endless stars, its' towns, its' people, its' freedoms. In Australia you have space to breathe, she felt.

She spoke of Australia with pride and longing.

Margrit told Fred she would be going back to Australia. Australia was home and if he wanted to marry her living in Australia was part of the deal.

Fred had a fractured childhood. His Swiss father and Austrian mother divorced when the children were young. In the period between the wars some Austrian women looked for Swiss husbands so they could remain in Switzerland.

After the divorce his mother soon discovered motherhood was not her thing and she put the three children into an orphanage in Chur, a small mountainous village.

She went back to work.

Not having access to his children and then having them put in an orphanage was too heartbreaking for his father.

He shot himself.

The boys remained in the system for some years while their sister was fostered by a rich family. She didn't get an easier road though as her adoptive parents tended to use her as cheap labour.

Because of his family background, and his willingness to travel, Fred was not averse to the idea of leaving Switzerland.

And then there was Margrit, of course.

They were engaged at Easter, 1957, and travelled two weeks later to England to sail on the Orsova, which having made its' maiden voyage in 1954, was bound for Australia.

Margrit had been in Switzerland 18 months. She was coming home.

Initially she fretted.

The Suez Canal was closed. How were they going to get to Australia?

The second Arab-Israel war erupted out of Egypt nationalising the Suez, thus freezing out British and French investors. Linking with Israel the British and French sought to protect their investment by invading the Sinai Peninsula.

Before it became a 'hot' war the U.S.A. and the Soviet Union stepped in making various threats and were able to de-escalate the situation.

Even in 1956 two-thirds of Europe's oil came via the 200km long Suez Canal.

Egypt wanted tolls on the Canal to pay for the Aswan Dam.

Margrit and Fred wanted safe passage on a British vessel to Australia.

They found a solution they could afford and travelled to England. Why not? Margrit had some English now and Fred had previously holidayed there.

Their voyage put them back on the first part of the course taken by John and Janet 105 years earlier, cruising down the west coast of Africa and around the Cape of Good Hope.

Then they headed to Colombo and turned back down the Indian Ocean to Australian shores.

Back they came.

Back to the land of women wearing curlers in their hair in Moorabool Street on Saturday morning, before going to the football in the afternoon and/or the Palais to dance Saturday night away.

Back to the land of the 6pm swill when too many men staggered home with a bottle in a brown paper bag.

Back to people laughing with Margrit over her pronunciation.

Back to those Australian people she was getting to know and understand.

Back to her emerging 'Australianness'.

And back Margrit came to her job at Myers in accounts.

Fred picked up a job at Elders, as a clerk in the wool stores in Geelong. His Swiss accounting credentials were not recognised in Australia.

He would spend his working life managing offices in wool broking firms.

There is something very Australian about that.

Margrit and Fred married in 1958. Margrit's married name became ....

Translated from Swiss-German into English her surname means 'snowball'. An odd name in an Australian context but what a nod to Swiss heritage.

A fourth generation Aussie, with a Scottish background, named Rob Roy, would definitely appreciate it.

I love it because it's the name my wife carried until our wedding day.

I also love that my father, as the fifth son, was named after the Australian river he was born beside (No, not Darling, Beardy Waters or even Wog Wog.) and his younger brother bears the name of a Sydney suburb (Not Tempe to which the family has a connection in the Mallee.).

Next step was to build a house.

Before Margrit married she had moved back into the family's house. Construction was not complete and the family needed board to help the process along. Susan had been basically giving her whole wage to this end, otherwise she too might have followed big sister's example.

Fine arts could still be pursued in Switzerland.

Susan worked in an office having missed a previous job because she was not Catholic. It took until the 1950s to finally start sorting out the whole Catholic – Protestant hangover from Europe thing. Thankfully Christian faith was losing its' embedded historic animosities.

Fred's and Margrit's house began to emerge out of a paddock on the northwest side of Geelong with the help of Oskar and Margrit's brothers. When the kitchen was finished and water tank installed they moved in. The rest of the house was boards running across bearers.

For Margrit it felt like they were living in an Australian version of the Wild West. A dirt track led to their incomplete house. There was no sewerage or mains water, no central heating, whitegoods although more readily available than four years previous, were still difficult to come by, and relying on public transport was 'iffy' at best.

A year and a half after living in their home the bus still did not always pass their emerging suburb if not enough people were aboard.

Having a passenger eight months pregnant gave the driver no pause for reconsideration. Margrit walked the 4-5kms home.

Prior to this pregnancy she had lost twins at five months and the hospital took them away without even telling her what sex they were.

A lot of actions taken by varying authorities in this era were motivated by benevolence, yet, somehow, they failed to be benevolent.

In 1962 Margrit and Fred became naturalised Australians but they had been Australianised well before then.

They knew if someone gave you directions and said 'it's not far mate' that could mean anything from 2kms to 62kms to whatever.

Fred gave similar directions.

That is Australia for you. It is definitely not Switzerland.

With children came the shift from speaking Swiss-German at home to only speaking English. The eldest daughter started school with only the English she learnt playing with kids in the neighbourhood.

At school she became fiercely Australian but pleased she had the language access to her parentage.

Like her aunt, Regina, she quickly adopted English thanks to the old Universal Grammar function in the brain going into overdrive.

Oskar died aged 75 after living 31 years as an Australian. His death rivals Johns, who was pitched headfirst into gravel from his dray. Oskar, sitting in a lounge room with his oldest two daughters, was laughing at a joke Margrit told, when he had a heart attack and died.

He literally died laughing.

Take that for first generation Australian one-upmanship John.

With his Swiss background Oskar had climbed mountains on different continents in his retirement. He died at zero altitude sitting in a chair.

Beyond the grave, I imagine, he thanked God for giving him the best send-off ever… family and laughter.

Trudi lived to 97 and for her final 55 years she called herself Australian.

CHAPTER FIVE

And what of the sixth-generation man, the commentator of this tale?

He married a third generation Australian. And now the generations in this story are interlocked.

But first let's note their respective sixties childhood.

At 3 she decided, with a boy who lived four doors down, to jump on their tricycles and ride to her grandmother's. She could only speak Swiss-German so the boy might not have known what he was letting himself in for. They were found by the police 3kms away, on an arterial road, almost at her grandmother's.

Nothing wrong with her sense of direction.

At 4 he decided to wander through some paddocks and see what he could find. He found a teenage girl who gave him a ride on her horse and a Choo-Choo Bar, thus starting his love affair with aniseed flavouring.

He was found by his parents after a great afternoon out.

The thought must have run through both their little brains if the world can throw up experiences like this why wouldn't you keep doing similar things.

These two incidents spark questions around the character of an Australian childhood imbedding in the next generation a desire to go, to look beyond our current horizons.

All kids seek to explore their world but often that world can remain small.

Does the air we breathe, here, tickle and tease the idea of getting out there and doing stuff?

A healthy percentage of Australians are struck by an impetus to see what is on offer, despite the rise of helicopter parenting.

Some markers for her sixties childhood included:

- live candles on the Christmas tree (until it caught fire one year)
- looking for lucky Sunny Boys to get a free one
- sharing a tiny bedroom with her sister
- swinging on the Hills Hoist clothesline
- walking with her grade to one of the kid's homes to watch man walk on the moon
- getting their first telephone making it possible to talk briefly with family in Switzerland
- playing backyard cricket with kids, mostly boys, from her street
- going to the shop with five cents and getting a bag of lollies
- growing up eating pasta and schnitzel not steak and spuds

- going to the Pix cinema without a parent. You bought a lolly necklace to watch the first movie and at interval you bought a Dixie Cup to eat during the second film.
- being sent, a number of times, to buy biscuits for the teachers from the shop a kilometre from school, when in Grade 3 and only 10 years old. (Maybe the teacher had heard about her escapade when she was three.)

Some markers for his sixties childhood included:

- fruit trees in the backyard and a passionfruit vine wrapped around an outside dunny
- the nightman with leather neck and shoulder pad removing the can and on one memorable occasion failing to clamp it firmly shut with the ensuing mess running from the side of his head to his shoes
- a coal/wood slow-combustion stove which ran all year because it was the only source of heat for the hot water
- the parental refrain 'go off and play just be home for tea'
- playing war with spud guns
- exploring abandoned houses, without vandalising
- climbing trees, especially cypress hedges because you could leap from one tree to the next
- building cubby houses, swimming in dams and roaming free and wide

- bananas, milk bottles, clinkers, buddies and the holy trio of the lolly shelf: liquorice blocks, aniseed balls and Choo-Choo Bars
- soft drink bottles returned to milk bars for extra lollies
- the government milk program in Primary Schools, which you drank even when half-curdled from sitting in the sun too long
- Billy Goggin and Polly Farmer visiting the school and inspiring participation in A.F.L. football
- A border collie who walked him to school, returning to wait for him at the end of the day

Their lives were partially shaped by the freedoms, the restrictions, the expectations of childhood.

Then came secondary school and, for him, university, after a half-baked attempt at working as a joiner over one summer. (I wonder where that came from? Any thoughts, John?)

He carried the doubts, angst and stumbles those years bring but one great stabiliser was discovering surfing the summer of his fifteenth year.

Surfing burgeoned into a consuming passion.

In Second Year Arts, he, along with two mates, started Deakin University's first surfing club.

Coming from an era of counter culture non-competitive surfing all three frowned on the emerging world surfing circuit as much as they frowned on wannabe surfers who drove Sandman Panel Vans and largely kept their surfboard bolted to the roof rack.

Soooooo……. Cool.

In their minds a competitive, time restricted performance, with points for certain moves, buffeted against the soul of surfing. You don't constrict surfing to a predetermined model. The best surfing session is where you are having the most fun.

Surfing is freestyle expressionism. It is fluid grace and synergy, it is muscle burning athleticism, it is art in flow and symmetry, it is individual but best shared with mates, it is sunrises and sunsets or whatever time of day the waves turn it on the best, it is board under arm looking out to corduroy lines on blue or green velvet with a smile creeping across your face.

Surfing is taking that first jack-knifing wave and carving a deep bottom turn to lay down so horizontal you can kiss the water. And you do because this is not a competition.

Spontaneity has its own reward.

Momentum keeps you glued to the board, so you drive vertical, smack the lip and launch into a late-drop-pit. The lip curls over your head. Your toes dig deeper into the board as you hurtle into shrinking daylight.

Then Neptune reaches out to pull you into his tumultuous washing-machine world.

You're consumed with the sheer joy of what just happened and a point score encapsulating a 'failure' to escape the tube remains a foreign construct.

Of course, the world has moved on from the decade that was 1965-75. Big wave surfing, sponsored expression sessions, YouTube wave discovery surfing, surfing in the Olympics are part of the diverse mix offering something for everyone. All ages and a higher percentage of females now surf and do their thing in the ocean.

Deakin Uni Surf Club was initially about discounted wetsuits and boards and free wax from the boys at Rip Curl who were beginning to emerge from their garage business.

Around the time of establishing the surf club was also the crunch time for where on earth he was headed in life. Arts was not leading him to a career he dreamed of.

Should he throw the board in the camper, head for Cactus and on to W.A.

The trouble was he knew life could not revolve solely around surfing. He had been unimpressed with his own behaviour on recent occasions, behaviour low on respect and high on floundering in emerging manhood.

Merging with this questioning of self was the surfing/hippie philosophy of life which held the tenet there is not enough humanity in humanity.

Violence and death seemed to be tools you pulled from your kit bag when required and the dollar trumped almost everything else in life.

Shock. Horror. Wham. This is when faith emerged.

A foundational question humanity seems to have been made to ask is: What will we anchor our lives to and where does that take us?

Redemption, love, good news, all solidified in the form of one foreign man in a foreign land with a very foreign culture 2000 years ago, who had three years of public ministry to make it clear who he was, why he was there at that time and what his coming and departure meant for humanity throughout time and in any culture.

Getting to know Him brought clarity for self and for people in general.

Embracing a love and faith that begins outside our makeup but somehow is birthed in our spirit, anchors our flimsy grip on life and propels us in previously unconsidered directions.

People can have a generational heritage where faith pops up (With my people it largely came under the Presbyterian umbrella.) but it is when faith becomes personal, individual, intimate and public that we own a gift of faith.

With faith and love came a marriage between a sixth and a third generation Australian.

This was the 1970's and she was 17.

Whoa! What? Slow down!

Was this some reversal on a 1950's 30-year-old obtaining a family arranged younger bride from the old country scenario?

No!!!!

At 17 she was a distributor for an overseas buyer, after leaving school at the end of Year 10. Determinedly independent and having a faith that was planted and grew from the age of 10, she was ready to embrace the next stage of life (and me.... thank goodness) even when it came earlier than expected. She wanted to build her life with her own family and was as ready as a 17-year-old can be.

Family started one year later. (Oh, in case you are still wondering, the age difference is four years.)

Through the childhood to teenage years, with four children in tow, she moved into part time work and then developed her own business. Being creative is part of her faith's expression, which was fashioned and enlarged over the years.

Thus, there were four children for the seventh generation, and then six children for the eighth generation.

Looks, quirks, mannerisms, talents etc might partially hearken back to previous generations but asking for grace does not come through family.

It comes like a wave with the ocean calling you to get on your feet and see where life can take you.

CHAPTER SIX

Late Spring

Oceans wrap the Australian coast in beauty, a wild beauty, a distinctly Australian charisma. John, Janet, Oskar and Trudi found their way here via the ocean, found a home which offered a distinctive life to succeeding generations, found a country which at its' best gives hope to the prodigal, to the searchers, in each generation.

Australia has the capacity to produce ensuing generations who say let's get on with shaping a better future, let's crack-on.

In a world bent out of shape, faith and love can go a long way to holding heads high, come what may.

The migrant experience teaches everyone to embrace change, to accept the previously unseen and the incomprehensible are part of life too.

Living in a unique country offers us so much.

It is good to be able to say 'I am, you are, we are Australian.'

www.ingramcontent.com/pod-product-compliance
Lightning Source LLC
La Vergne TN
LVHW050937080826
845145LV00004B/1305

* 9 7 8 1 7 6 4 2 8 1 3 0 0 *